DISC

Action Sports

Tae Kwon Do

Bill Gutman

Illustrated with Photographs
by Peter Ford

Capstone Press

MINNEAPOLIS

Printed in the United States of America.

Capstone Press • 2440 Fernbrook Lane • Minneapolis, MN 55447

Editorial Director   John Coughlan
Managing Editor   John Martin
Production Editor   James Stapleton
Copy Editor   Thomas Streissguth

Library of Congress Cataloging-in-Publication Data

Gutman, Bill.
    Tae kwon do / Bill Gutman.
        p.   cm.
    Includes bibliographical references and index.
    Summary: Describes the kicking and striking techniques of tae kwon do, originally a Korean art, now a worldwide sport. Includes a glossary of terms.
    ISBN 1-56065-266-7
    1. Tae kwon do--Juvenile literature.   [1. Tae kwon do.]
I. Title
    GV1114.9.G88 1996
    796.8'153--dc20   95-7809
                                                          CIP
                                                          AC

99 98 97   6 5 4 3 2

Table of Contents

Chapter 1

The Art of Striking with the Feet and Fists

Tae Kwon Do is the art of striking with the feet and fists. In the Korean language, "Tae" means to kick or strike with the foot. "Kwon" means to punch or strike with the fist. "Do" means art or skill.

Tae Kwon Do is different from other martial arts. There is a wide range of kicking techniques. There is also an emphasis on breaking objects with the fist. In Tae Kwon Do, many spinning and leaping kicks are delivered through the air. And they are dazzling.

Tae Kwon Do is a Korean form of martial arts that goes back more than 1,000 years. The modern form of the art began about 1910. That's when both Chinese and Japanese empty-hand techniques became part of the form. It has been called Tae Kwon Do only since about 1945.

In 1973, the **World Taekwon-do Federation** (WTF) was formed. That same year the first World Tae Kwon Do championships were held in Seoul, Korea.

A Worldwide Sport

Today, Tae Kwon Do is practiced all over the world. The sport was demonstrated at the 1988 Summer Olympics at Seoul in South Korea.

As with other forms of martial arts, those practicing Tae Kwon Do wear **colored belts** to

Tae Kwon Do teaches ways to attack and defend.

show the skill level they have reached. Beginners wear white belts, followed by gold, green, blue, brown, and black belts. There are, in fact, two levels each of gold, green, blue, and brown belt. There are nine levels of black belt.

The clothing worn for Tae Kwon Do is a loose-fitting white cotton outfit, similar to that worn for karate, In recent years, many people have begun wearing a slipover top of the same cut and length and the traditional wrapover jacket.

Powerful kicks and skillful blocks with the hands and arms are the heart of Tae Kwon Do.

Chapter 2
Getting Ready

Tae Kwon Do is not a sport or art to be taken lightly. Someone skilled in the art can seriously injure an unsuspecting person. It is not the object of Tae Kwon Do or any martial art to injure someone. An unskilled and untrained person who tries some of the difficult kicks of Tae Kwon Do or tries breaking bricks can seriously injure himself.

A person getting ready to study Tae Kwon Do should be in good physical condition when he begins. You can pre-train by doing an aerobic exercise like jogging, swimming, biking, or jumping rope. And you can work on toning other muscles by doing pushups, situps, and pullups.

Stretching

To excel at Tae Kwon Do, your body must be flexible. The spins, leaps, and high kicks demand it. Even advanced black belts go through a long warmup period of stretching. This gets the muscles in the legs, hips, and back loose and flexible. Muscles must be

The right stance and positioning allows you to attack or defend instantly.

Stretching exercises prepare your muscles for the tough workout ahead.

stretched regularly or they will begin to tighten.

A Few Warmup Stretches

Here are a few basic **stretching** exercises that will get your muscles ready for Tae Kwon Do. Stretching exercises should be done slowly. Muscles should be held in the stretched

position for five to ten seconds, then released slowly. Do not stretch a muscle beyond the point where you begin to feel pain or discomfort.

A good regular stretch is called the split stretch. It is done with your feet spread wide apart, the legs straight. While bending at the waist, touch the right hand to the left toe, then the left hand to the right toe. In between, stand straight up. Soon you will be able to stretch your feet wider and wider apart.

The hamstring stretch is another good one. (The hamstring is located at the back of the thigh. It gets a real workout during Tae Kwon Do moves.) In this stretch, find a bar or bench about waist high. Place one leg on the support, keeping it straight. Bend your other leg slightly at the knee and lean forward slowly over the leg on the support. As you slide your hands toward your foot, you will feel the hamstring stretch.

Stretching exercises get students ready for the tough workout ahead.

A good exercise to loosen both the backs of the legs and the lower back is the hurdler's stretch. This is done by sitting with your legs spread wide apart in front. Fold one leg back until it is tucked tight to the buttocks. Next, rock forward from the waist, stretching your hands toward the foot of the outstretched leg. Hold and repeat five times before switching to the other leg.

Students help each oither in a Tae Kwon Do class.

Chapter 3

Kicking and Striking

Tae Kwon Do has been called a method of self-defense without weapons. Like other martial arts, it combines both mind and body. The mind must be relaxed, yet alert. It must be able to see what an opponent is going to do quickly. This allows the body to react in a split second. This kind of concentration and focus takes time to perfect.

Developing Striking Force

Tae Kwon Do is basically a kicking art. The legs are the most powerful natural weapons a person has for defending himself.

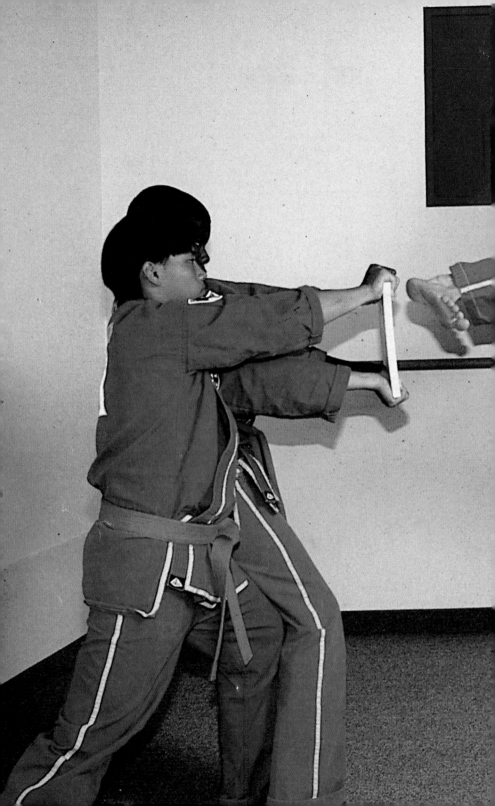

In Tae Kwon Do kicks, the leg is like a coiled spring that is suddenly released. The muscles provide power. The joints (hip, knee, ankle) give a spring-like snap that leads to maximum power at the point of impact.

There are two kinds of kicking techniques in Tae Kwon Do—direct and circular. The **direct kick** moves in a straight line from the kicker to the target. This can be a **front kick, side kick, back kick,** or a leaping kick. The **circular kick** moves in any direction other than straight. There are a number of spinning and **roundhouse kicks.**

Arms and Shoulders

Even though much of Tae Kwon Do involves kicks, there are striking techniques with the arms and hands like those used in karate. You should have the same kind of snapping and springing strike force with your arms as you have with your legs.

It is important to develop strength and power in your shoulders and arms. The snap

Leaping kicks take good timing and lots of practice.

comes from the shoulders, elbows, and wrists.
You use your arms to block kicks and punches.
It takes strength in the arms to block a
powerful kick.

In Tae Kwon Do, strength, speed, and
flexibility are all important. With training and
practice, you will improve in each area.

23

Chapter 4
Practicing Kicks

Many Tae Kwon Do kicks are aimed at head level, so it is necessary to aim high with the kicking foot. Both direct and circular kicks can be delivered in two ways. The first is with one foot planted firmly on the ground. The other is in the air, either leaping or spinning.

Most kicks in Tae Kwon Do are delivered from a **back stance.** In this stance, from 60 to 80 percent of the body's weight is on the back leg. The front foot points toward the target. The toes of the rear foot angle outward at 45 to 90 degrees.

This is the method for making all Tae Kwon Do kicks. Of course, with leaping and flying kicks, the rear foot does not remain planted. The body and leg must generate their power in the air.

The Front Kick

The front kick is delivered from directly in front of an opponent. The leg is thrust straight out, springing toward the target.

The same basic rules apply as in other Tae Kwon Do kicks. Use the back stance for leverage. The hands should be held about chest high, with the fists clenched. That way, you're ready to block a kick from your opponent. The kicking leg must move quickly. And the body should be relaxed so that it can explode with power.

The next movements should be made very quickly, so that it appears as one explosive action. First, the knee must be raised. At the same time, shift a good part of your weight to the back foot, your back knee bent slightly. Point your foot at the target, then snap your leg forward using both hip and knee to generate power.

A flying front kick is delivered with the ball of the foot pointed at the target.

You make contact with the ball of your foot. If you make contact with your toes, you may injure them.

The Flying Front Kick

The same kind of snap and power is generated with a flying front kick. But it's done while leaping in the air. This time, the back leg is drawn up at the knee as the front leg completes the kick.

The Side Kick

The side kick is another direct kick, going straight to the target. The main difference is that the body is turned sideways, or at a 90-degree angle to the target. The kicking leg is raised sideways. The snap of the lower leg and foot also comes from the side to the target.

The Back Kick

The basic back kick is delivered with the same technique. It is also a direct kick. This time, the kick is made with your back to the target. Lean forward, shifting much of your weight to the front foot. Your kicking leg is raised behind you. Your foot points to the target as the kick is snapped off.

Roundhouse and Spin Kicks

These are examples of the circular kicks of Tae Kwon Do. They are not direct kicks. The leg sweeps across in an arc, hitting the target from the side.

Great flexibility is needed for the leg to make the arc quickly and powerfully. In a

Two feet allow you to take on two attackers.

roundhouse kick with the right leg, the leg sweeps right to left. The kick is delivered with much of the weight still shifted to the back foot. Instead of being brought forward, the leg is raised out to the right, the knee high.

As the leg is raised right, lean left at the waist to maintain your balance. The kick is delivered across the body, your foot parallel to the ground and your toes pointed left. The leg must generate power and snap at the point of impact. This takes practice.

Timing

Roundhouse, spin, and flying kicks are the most spectacular in Tae Kwon Do. It takes a lot of practice to learn these techniques and put them into action. Working with a coach or in a class is the best way to learn.

To deliver a spinning roundhouse kick, for instance, you have to know just what you're doing. The distance between you and your opponent must be just right. You must then spin a full 360 degrees, turning completely around. As you come out of the spin your lead leg must already be in the air. Your balance has to be perfect.

You have to pick up the target in a split second, point with your foot and drive the kick into the target. If you miss, you will be open for a counter-attack. Or you may lose your balance. It takes a great deal of timing to deliver the kick properly.

Chapter 5

Punching and Blocking

Although Tae Kwon Do is thought of as mainly a kicking discipline, there are also punching techniques similar to those of karate.

Punching
Punches are delivered mainly with the fist. Each punch should be delivered with maximum force.

The Sparring Stance
Before getting ready to launch a punch, opponents square off in a sparring stance. It is like the stance two boxers take when squaring off against each other. The stance is wide, one

leg in front of the other, knees slightly bent. Arms are held chest high, fists clenched. The lead arm–the same as the lead leg–is held out in front of the body, the other arm back against the chest.

Direct Punches

Most punches are direct, straightahead blows. Your body should remain straight. Arm and leg should be thrust forward at the same time. If you're punching with the left hand, then thrust your left leg forward at the same time. The front foot should point directly at the target, the rear foot outward at about a 45-degree angle.

The arm and fist are thrust out in a straight and compact, but powerful, movement. At the point of impact, the wrist is twisted downward to make the blow even more powerful.

Roundhouse Punches

Most Tae Kwon Do punches are direct. But some are thrown in a roundhouse style. The spinning backhand punch is one of these. It is thrown using the same technique as the spinning, roundhouse kick. This time it is the extended arm that targets the opponent instead of the leg.

Once again, timing and distance are very important. Before making a 360-degree spin, make sure you are close enough to reach your opponent. Otherwise, you may be punching the air.

Blocking Techniques

In Tae Kwon Do, as in other martial arts, no one is going to stand still to be hit or kicked. They will try to stop the blow so they can launch a blow of their own. Both the arms and legs can be used for **blocking.**

Kicks aimed at the head can by blocked by crossing the forearms in front of the face. Always keep the fists clenched to avoid injury to the fingers. Punches can be blocked the same way, or with a single arm.

Another way to block a flying kick is to deflect the kicking foot with your elbow and

Opponents square off to deliver their punches. Arm and fist move together to deliver a powerful blow.

upper arm. This is done with the fists clenched and held close to the body. Lean your head back and raise your arm at the elbow to deflect the kick. This technique takes timing and practice.

There are a number of other basic blocking positions, using both the arms and legs. You will learn these as you continue to study Tae Kwon Do.

Chapter 6

Competition

There are various kinds of competitions in Tae Kwon Do, ranging from **no-contact** to **light-contact** and, in some cases, to **full-contact**. In no-contact competition, points are awarded for a good punch or kick that, in the eyes of the referee, would have connected with the target. No one gets hurt by the powerful kicks and punches.

Light-contact competition allows the blows to land, but without full force. Competitors must learn to pull their punches and kicks so they don't land solidly. It takes skill and practice to do this right. Contests can still be exciting and very competitive. And injuries are kept to a minimum.

Full-Contact Tae Kwon Do

Tae Kwon Do can be a very fierce form of martial arts. Experts in the sport wanted to test themselves against others without pulling punches. But something was needed to prevent injuries.

The answer was **body armor.** Safety equipment and body armor began to appear in the 1970s. By the time Tae Kwon Do appeared as a demonstration sport in the 1988 Olympics, body armor had made full-contact competition possible.

Full-contact is very exciting. Opponents wear padded gloves, boots, chest and rib protectors, and headguards. With this gear, there could be full-contact Tae Kwon Do with little risk of serious injury. This kind of body armor is available to everyone. If you want to practice full-contact, be sure to wear it.

Breaking Bricks and Boards

Almost everyone has seen Tae Kwon Do experts amaze their audiences by breaking bricks and thick boards. This is done with a single blow from the hands or feet. It takes great practice and concentration to generate enough power to do this.

This is something that should not be taken lightly. Do not try this on your own. You might cause serious injury to your hand, wrist, foot, or ankle. If you want to learn how to break bricks and boards, seek instruction from a Tae Kwon Do expert qualified in this technique.

Learn slowly and correctly. That way, you'll find out if you can master the technique with minimal risk of injury.

Tae Kwon Do is an exciting form of martial arts. It can help you get in great physical condition. It can also help you gain self-confidence. But you should always remember that the skill and power you gain in Tae Kwon Do should not be abused.

Glossary

back kick–a basic Tae Kwon Do kick. The back kick is a direct kick delivered with your back to the target.

back stance–the position from which most Tae Kwon Do kicks are delivered. The kick is made from a stance that puts 60 to 80 percent of the weight on the back, or supporting, leg.

blocking–stopping a punch, kick, or any attacking move by an opponent

body armor–protective gear that allows full-contact Tae Kwon Do competition while keeping injuries to a minimum

circular kick–a kick that approaches the target from the side, rather than on a straight line from the kicker to the target

colored belts–the means by which the skill level of someone studying Tae Kwon Do is indicated. A white belt indicates a beginner. The most skilled fighters wear black belts. There are other colored belts between the white belt and the black belt. Belts are always worn during workouts, classes, and competitions.

direct kick–a kick that approaches the target in a straight line from the kicker to the target. It may be a front, back, or side kick.

front kick–a direct kick made directly in front of an opponent. It travels straight from the kicker to the target.

full-contact Tae Kwon Do–competition that allows opponents to kick and punch each other with full force

light-contact Tae Kwon Do–competition in which only light contact is allowed. It can test the skills of opponents without the risk of injury or the need for body armor.

no-contact Tae Kwon Do–competition in which no contact is allowed. Points are given for punches and kicks which would have landed.

Opponents must have the skill to make their moves without making contact.

roundhouse kick–a circular kick in which the leg sweeps through the air and makes contact with the target from the side

sidekick–a kick in which the body is turned sideways at a 90-degree angle to the target. The kicking leg is raised sideways.

stretching–warm-up exercises which increase flexibility in the muscles and joints

World Taekwon-do Federation (WTF)–the worldwide organization that governs and controls the sport of Tae Kwon Do

To Learn More

Barrett, Norman. *The Martial Arts.* New York: F. Watts, 1988.

Craven, Jerry. *Tae Kwon Do.* Vero Beach, Florida: Rourke, 1994.

You can read articles about Tae Kwon Do in *Tae Kwon Do Times, Inside Tae Kwon Do*, and *Taekwondo World.*

Acknowledgment

A special thanks to National Karate Schools for their ongoing cooperation.

Some Useful Addresses

World Taekwon-do Federation (WTF)
635, Yuksam-dong
Kangnam-ku
Seoul, Korea 135

United States Taekwon-do Union
1750 E. Boulder Street
Colorado Springs, CO 80909

WTF Taekwondo Association of Canada
3078 Winston Church Boulevard
Mississauga, Ontario, Canada S7L 6H4

United States Taekwon-Do Federation
6801 W. 117th Ave. E-5
Broomfield, CO 80020

Index